THE RODIN MUSEUM GUIDE

THE
RODIN MUSEUM
GUIDE

IN THE HÔTEL BIRON

Monique Laurent

Photographs by
Bruno Jarret

LES GUIDES VISUELS

HAZAN

© 1994, Éditions Hazan

Cover illustration:
Orphée et les Ménades

Translated by Jane Roberts

Photoengraving: Blanchard, Paris

ISBN. 2 85025 36 26
ISSN. 1151 8502

Printed in France

The Hôtel Biron from the courtyard

THE HÔTEL BIRON
AND THE RODIN MUSEUM

Among the great houses in the Rue de Varenne described in the guides of the eighteenth century as the "most remarkable of the realm", the Hôtel Biron, which became the Musée Rodin after the First World War, is one of the most beautiful, with the added charms of its magnificent gardens.

In 1728, Abraham Perenc de Moras, a lowly born but ambitious and entrepreneurial businessman, had made a large fortune speculating in paper money and was able to build his "hôtel" in a quarter only recently urbanized, near the royal foundation of the Invalides, "the most magnificent House in Paris". Its plans are attributed to Jacques Gabriel, Royal Inspector of the King's Buildings, with whom Perenc de Moras had had several property deal-

ings, in particular in the Place Louis Le Grand, now the Place Vendôme. The project was actually carried out by another architect, Jean Aubert, who had designed the very grand Stables of the Château de Chantilly and had worked on the Palais Bourbon, now home of the National Assembly.

The rapidity of the realization of the project – only three years – probably accounts for the general harmony of the building which is a prime example of the Rococo or "Rocaille" style which flourished in the first quarter of the eighteenth century and whose characteristics are particularly visible on the garden façade with its central balcony resting on intricate stone brackets and the mask and shell motifs over each window.

Perenc de Moras died in 1731 without having had time to take advantage of his magnificent residence, only recently completed.

His widow let it to the Duchesse de Maine, King Louis XIV's daughter-in-law, who ended her turbulent life of intrigue here in 1753 at the age of 78. Perenc's descendants then sold the property to the Duc de Biron whose name henceforth it bore. The duke was a Grand Marshal of France and a peer of the realm and as well as being a very brave warrior and hero of Louis XV's campaigns, he also loved splendour and made the Hôtel famous for its lavish feasts and celebrations held in the gardens where Parisian promenaders were admitted. In 1782, he entertained the Grand Duke of Russia, who was to become Tsar Paul, and his wife, who were travelling through Europe under the somewhat transparent pseudonym of "Count and Countess of the North"!

After the old duke's death in 1788, his nephew the Duc de Lauzun inherited the Hôtel. After having spent some years in scandalous pursuits at Court, he left for America to fight in the War of Independence, finally to become a commander of the French Revolutionary forces which didn't prevent him, for all his modern ideas, from being guillotined in 1793!

Like most aristocratic residences during the Revolution, the Hôtel Biron was abandoned for several years. Under the Directory, the property was let to a contractor who specialized in public fêtes, balls and picnics, concerts, fireworks, performances by acrobats and magicians and even hot air balloon rides, transforming the beautiful gardens into a fairground!

During the Consulate and the Empire, it became the residence of slightly more austere inhabitants in the form of the Papal Legation and then the Russian Ambassador, Prince Kourakine.

The owner at this time was the elderly and pious Duchesse de Charost who, concerned that the house should go to a properly devout cause, sold it to the Holy Society of the Sacred Heart of Jesus, founded in 1804 by Mother Sophie Barat to educate the young daughters of the French and foreign aristocracy. For nearly a century, the convent of the Mothers of the Sacred Heart provided an excellent education to young boarders and novices whose social rank assured the school a prestigious reputation

Unfortunately, the rules of the convent which aimed at protecting its pupils from the frivolous and worldly, caused the order to strip the building of its interior including the overdoors by Lemoyne and Coypel, the mirrors over the fireplaces, the sumptuous panelling and gilded carving, the intricate wrought-iron balconies and railings: all were dispersed and whatever you see now is the fruit of patient research, tracking down and careful negotiating to buy back and restore certain features to their original state.

In 1904, the law which separated the powers of the State and the Church led to the closure of the boarding school and the receiver of the bankrupt Order decided to let out some space very cheaply in the abandoned buildings while deciding whether to sell it on or demolish. The Hôtel Biron was finally saved because the "apartments" were in fact hastily and unofficially rented out to artists attracted by the strange charm of an empty "palace". Jean Cocteau described it in his *Portraits Souvenirs* but many others lived there including Matisse, the actor De Max, the American dancer Isadora Duncan and most significantly the German poet Rainer Maria Rilke who persuaded Rodin to move in.

The sculptor, who was at this time at the height of international fame, kept his home at the Villa des Brillants in Meudon where he had his workshops and where his wife, Rose Beuret, resided but he came every day to the Hôtel Biron to entertain his friends, to draw, to add to his considerable personal art collection and to wander through the gardens which had become wild and overgrown.

The property was finally purchased by the State in 1911 and a part of the garden was relinquished to create the playgrounds of the Lycée Victor Duruy, but the future of the Hôtel still remained uncertain: this allowed public opinion aided by Rodin's friends and admirers to suggest the creation of a museum in the Hôtel Biron dedicated to the great artist: no easy task, it seems, involving petitions and political interventions by the likes of Poincaré, Clemenceau, Barrès, Clémentel and support from artists such as Monet, Mirbeau, Debussy and Romain Rolland, because not only was Rodin's work still controversial and attracting hostility from influential circles but the French State seemed reluctant to dedicate a national museum to a living artist. The outbreak of the First World War delayed the conclusion of the debate until 1916. Meanwhile, Rodin had been organizing his estate and, in 1916, he gave the French State, in three successive donations, the bulk of his collections, his personal archives, his property in Meudon and, above all, the whole of his "oeuvre" complete with reproduction rights. He died the following year.

In 1919, the Hôtel Biron was opened to the public as a national museum and is now one of the most frequented in Paris. The visitor should also go to the Musée Rodin in Meudon (Villa des Brillants) where initial terracottas and original plasters for the major works are exhibited: these serve to explain fully the working techniques of the artist. Rodin is buried next to Rose Beuret, his wife, in the gardens of this villa.

The Hôtel Biron from the gardens

Mignon

THE MUSEUM

Your visit begins on the left of the entrance hall after crossing the sales area which was formerly the dining-room of the Hôtel Biron.

ANTE-ROOM. This room contains the very first sculpted busts by Rodin: the portrait of his father, Jean-Baptiste Rodin, in a truly classical style and also that of R.P. Eymard, who was founder of the Pères du Très-Saint-Sacrement where Rodin spent some time during a religious crisis he underwent in 1863.

ROOM 1. This room concentrates on works, mainly portraits, of between 1860 and 1870. Some are decorative busts in a fanciful eighteenth century style, such as *Diane* and *Dosia*, typical examples of the rather sentimental sculpture hugely popular at this time with the bourgeois clientèle, others are in a more realistic style, such as the effigies of Monsieur and Madame Garnier. These last pieces manage at last to reconcile the likeness of the model with a very personal technique :

The Man with the Broken Nose

Young Girl in a Flowered Hat

it is doubtful today, as was widely believed, whether *Mignon* is in fact the portrait of Rose Beuret, Rodin's companion: the title was more probably inspired by the then very fashionable opera of the same name by Ambroise Thomas. In the terracotta *Young Girl in a Flowered Hat*, Rodin contrasts with great panache the velvet of the model's skin with the intricate complexity of her hat and hair. With *The Man with the Broken Nose*, he manages to portray the terribly mutilated face of his model with the dignified grandeur of the classical Greek busts of philosophers which Rodin had no doubt studied at the Louvre. Before this marble, Rodin had executed the same subject in terracotta which had curiously been refused by the Salon as too trivial.

On the walls, Rodin's and his friend Barnouvin's oil portraits recall the artist's friends and relatives.

Young Woman with a Child

ROOM 2. Most of the works in this room were executed while Rodin worked as an assistant for Carrier-Belleuse who was the most successful sculptor of the Second Empire. Thus, the base of the planter called *Vasque des Titans*, because of its muscular figures inspired by Michelangelo, is signed by Carrier-Belleuse although we know that it was in fact done by Rodin.

From 1871 to 1877, Rodin resided in Brussels where he helped his eminent employer with important commissions for public buildings and monuments while trying to sell his own sculptures which were very much in the vein of the period, in a pleasing and animated style, examples of which are exhibited here such as *Bacchante, The Idyll of Ixelles, The Spring, Children with a Lizard* and *Young Woman with a Child*. We could probably recognize in

Brother and Sister

Bacchante

The Spring

the rounded and rather hesitant features of Rodin's children at this time the son borne by Rose Beuret in 1866 whom he never admitted was his own. During his "Belgian" period, he pursued his work as a portraitist and used his friends as models, such as Paul de Vigne, a sculptor, whose pleasant and relaxed expression contrasts strongly with the conservative and stern realism used to portray Alexander van Beckelaer, a chemist who had lent him money. The squared-up study of Rubens' *Descent from the Cross* and the oil studies of the surrounding areas of Brussels show that Rodin used his stay in Belgium to extend his artistic education by copying Old Masters and painting "on the motif" in the surrounding countryside.

A display case contains some decorative designs created by Rodin for the Sèvres porcelain factory where he worked from time to time between 1879 and 1882, thanks once again to Carrier-Belleuse who had become director there.

Children with a Lizard

The Idyll of Ixelles

The Age of Bronze

ROOM 3. Formerly the Oval Drawing Room or the Great East Chamber, this charming room has thankfully at last recovered its unpainted carved panelling, which had been painted white with gilded details, its overmantel mirrors and its mythological overdoors (copies of the originals unfortunately still missing).

The Age of Bronze was the first life-size figure Rodin executed after a trip to Italy where he was literally bowled over by the sculptures of Michelangelo and it is a mixture of the careful study of nature and the strong influence of the Italian Renaissance. Exhibited at the Paris Salon of 1877, the anatomy of his model seemed so lifelike compared to the lifeless Academic efforts of the time that Rodin was accused of having cast his sculptures directly on the living model! The resulting scandal attracted widespread attention to Rodin who decided to return to Paris to fulfil his ambitions and various new projects. *The Call to Arms* is the work submitted by the artist for the competition organized in 1879 for a monument commemorating the defence of Paris during the Franco-Prussian war. It consists of a dying soldier dominated by the Spirit of War calling him to arms. It was judged too violent and lacking in dignity and was never considered by the jury.

Rodin also started the series of portraits of other artists which he was to pursue throughout his career: the bust of Carrier-Belleuse is tribute of sorts to his former employer and has the sensitivity and expressive qualities of an eighteenth century portrait. The busts of the painters J.P.Laurens and Alphonse Legros, who taught Rodin the techniques of print-making, and of Jules Dalou, one of the best sculptors of the Third Republic, are more classically rendered. Among the feminine subjects, *Madame Roll* was the wife of the reputable painter, Alfred Roll, and in *Madame A.C.* (it was usual to designate ladies of social standing by discreet initials only!), we must probably recognize the wife of the fashionable decorator Victor-Michel Cruchet.

The Call to Arms

The Call to Arms

Madame A.C. (Madame Cruchet)

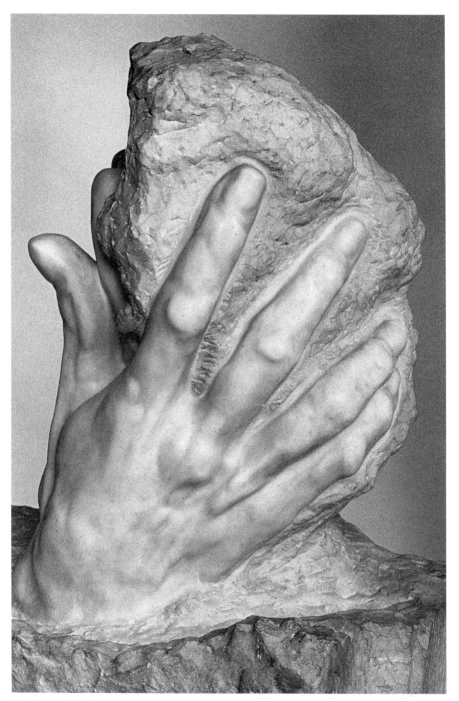

The Hand of God

ROOM 4. In the middle of this room, which served as antechamber of the officers of the Duchesse de Maine, stands the monumental marble *The Hand of God*, a particularly symbolic work because it evokes not only the divine power creating man out of dust but also the hand of the artist modelling clay. The representation of God as a large hand seems to have been inspired by medieval painting in which God is often portrayed as a hand appearing from a cloud. In fact, Rodin re-used the hand of one of the *Burghers of Calais* (see ROOM 11): this way of modifying dramatically the meaning of a piece by using it in a different context is a fundamental characteristic of Rodin's art. The seemingly inexhaustible theme of the couple which allows him to express all the nuances of human passion can be seen in this room : *Eternal Spring*, which can be related to the series of *The Kiss* in the next room, was so popular because of its youthful theme that it was reproduced over and over again in bronze. The same womanly form can be recognized as part of *Illusions Received by the Earth*, yet another symbol of human dreams devoured by earthly forces. In *The Eternal Idol*, Rodin explores other subtle feelings between man and woman: in a somewhat triangular composition, he expresses the overpowering beauty of the woman and her indifference towards her adoring partner. *Earth and Moon* has had other titles – *Sun and Moon* or *Soul Leaving the Body* for instance – and represents two figures hardly freed from the block of marble but still attached to it by surfaces treated like wavy hair or stylized waves. *Paolo and*

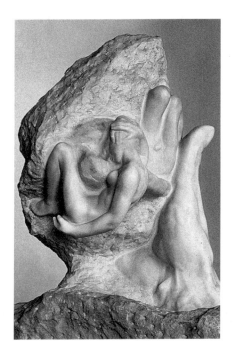

The Hand of God

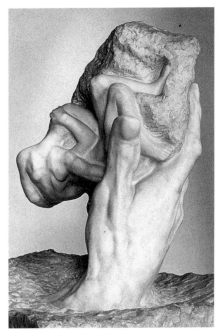

Francesca is a subject taken from Dante's *Inferno*, and the particular poem which tells of the adulterous love of Paolo Malatesta for his sister-in-law Francesca di Rimini, and illustrates to the full Rodin's original technique of contrasting the highly polished figures with the crude roughness of the block of marble. In complete contrast, the severe and static marble portrait of Rose Beuret, who would only become Rodin's wife in 1917, is by the artist Antoine Bourdelle who himself became one of the most famous sculptors of the first half of the twentieth century.

On the mantelpiece of the fireplace, *Pallas with the Parthenon* was inspired by the beautiful but rather

Illusions Received by the Earth

expressionless face of Marianne Russell, who was the wife of the Australian painter John Russell. The little Greek temple in plaster in the marble hair explains the curious title.

The pictures in this room come from the artist's private collection, and particularly remarkable are the paintings by Eugène Carrière whom Rodin much admired (see also the next room) and the powerful and sombre still-life by the artist Théodule Ribot.

Paolo and Francesca

Eternal Spring

The Eternal Idol

The Eternal Idol

The Prayer; Large torso of a man; Torso of a woman

ROOM 5. The great central hall, the main reception room of the Hôtel, divides the two ground-floor wings facing the garden. One of the original overdoor panels by Lemoyne, *Venus and the Three Graces*, was recently returned to its proper place.

In this room, some of the artist's very well-known pieces are exhibited as if to show the extraordinary variety with which Rodin treats the human form as a theme. *The Kiss*, which was conceived as part of *The Gates of Hell* (see : ROOMS 9 and 10 and the GARDENS) to illustrate the love between Paolo and Francesca, is one of the most famous sculptures in the world: its entwined and passionately embracing figures represent to this day a symbol of erotic art. In contrast to this complex but somewhat static composition, *Torso of a woman (half-length)* seems to emit an astonishing dynamic force which is also present in *Iris, Messenger of the Gods*: this figure seems to be floating in mid-air in an extremely daring pose.

In other cases, such as in *The Prayer*, the *Large torso of a man* and the *Torso of a woman*, which are shown against the backdrop of a copy of Rembrandt's *Bethsheba* by Ricard, they are shown fully-frontal, headless and armless and recall the Greek and Roman antiquities which Rodin collected often in a damaged condition. He can be seen as an innovator in portraying the human form in as much that he not only fragments the forms but, by repeating them in an unexpected fashion, creates new rhythms in space. *The Cathedral* is a subtle example of this technique: it is composed of what looks like a pair of upwardly stretched hands, but in fact, we do not even notice that the artist has used the same right hand twice so as to avoid the monotony and symmetry of corresponding fingers and thumbs. Despite its title inspired by Gothic vaulting, *The Cathedral* was in fact a project for a fountain. *The Secret* is another example of this curious "assemblage" of hands.

The Prayer

Torso of a woman (half-length)

The Kiss

Large torso of a man

The Cathedral

Aurora

ROOM 6. This magnificent partially restored panelled drawing room was once the Duchesse de Maine's formal reception room. Here one can see works by Rodin inspired by Camille Claudel as well as a number of works by Camille Claudel herself. She was not only his most eminent pupil but also his mistress and inspiration for many years before she was declared insane at the age of 48 and locked away in an asylum until her death thirty years later.

Among Rodin's works, which recent research has shown were nearly all executed just before or during the break-up of their relationship in 1892, one must note *Farewell*, composed of a youthful head with close-cropped hair and two oddly assorted hands on a base, and *Aurora*, with the melancholic face of Camille looming up out of the rough block of marble. Of *The Conva-* *lescent*, Madame Nicole Barbier, author of the catalogue of Rodin's marble works, notes that its face and hands seem to sink into the marble as one might descend into madness. In a display case, one can view a version of a small plaster in molten glass, a very old technique which had recently been re-discovered by artists at the beginning of the twentieth century, and a curious "assemblage" of a portrait head of Camille combined with a hand taken from *The Burghers of Calais*.

To the left of the door, *Galatea* strangely resembles a work by Camille, *Girl with a Sheaf* (not in this Museum's collections), and could have very well been executed by her in Rodin's workshop and only signed by the master.

Camille Claudel's sculptures possess some of the lyrical and artistic qualities of Rodin's work but they also have

Camille Claudel: *The Conversation*

Camille Claudel: *Vertumnus and Pomona*

a very distinct personality and genius of their own. For instance, *Vertumnus and Pomona*, which is often compared to *The Eternal Idol* or *The Kiss* (in ROOMS 4 and 5), is a much more restrained and controlled work. In *The Waltz*, she depicts the dancing couple, not as an elegantly formal pair, but slightly off-balance, in a whirl of unbridled passion. *The Age of Maturity*, of which both the initial version in plaster and the final one in bronze are exhibited here, is purely autobiographical, showing the imploring Camille at the feet of an ageing Rodin protected by his elderly partner whom he will never be persuaded to abandon. The stylistic freedom of Camille is virtually explosive in *The Conversation*, executed in a greenish onyx marble, very difficult to work and often seen in Art Nouveau pieces, which gives it a strange charm not visible in the bronze (in the display case). It portrays four very small figures exchanging secrets in a rather run-of-the-mill, ordinary scene very far from Rodin's grand inspiration.

She was also a very vivid portraitist who went far beyond simple likeness. Of her portrait of Rodin which she sculpted in 1888, the Swiss critic Mathias Morhardt wrote: "It is a severe work ... whichever way you look at it, his profiles are always true, without faults or corrections, or indeed any hesitation". In *The Little Lady of the Manor*, she captures the fervent and intense Joan of Arc-like expression of the child who posed for her during a trip to Touraine. On the mantelpiece sits the bust of Paul Claudel, aged 37, her beloved younger brother, who was not only a diplomat of note but a celebrated playwright.

Camille Claudel in a Phrygian Cap

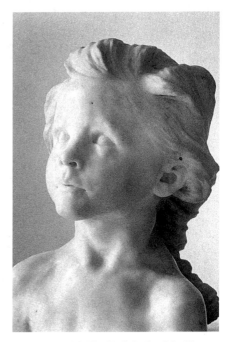

Camille Claudel: *The Little Lady of the Manor*

Camille Claudel: *The Age of Maturity*

Eve; on the mantelpiece, *Study of a woman*

ROOM 7. The panelling in this room, once the Great West Chamber or Oval Drawing Room, is particularly intricate, especially the marvellous carving of palm tree leaves around the overmantel mirrors, which are attributed to the interior designer Nicolas Pineau who worked at Versailles and in several other royal residences as well as at Peterhof, the summer residence of Peter the Great of Russia near Saint Petersburg. One of the decorative panels which belonged to the decor has recently been recovered and represents the Labours of Penelope.

The room is dominated by the life-size figure of *Eve*, the first large female representation in bronze made by Rodin which was meant to be placed on one side of *The Gates of Hell* with *Adam* on the other (see: the GARDENS); this was a popular subject at the time because of its obvious sensuality. Rodin is said to have used his usual model, a Mrs Abruzzezzi, and having realized that she was expecting a child, to have had to modify her shape so frequently that he decided to leave the area of her stomach rough and unfinished, an unusual technique for the times; the heel-piece, a support which helped the model to rest her bended leg, is kept by Rodin to give the bronze a counterbalance and a sense of harmony: this feature, as well as the preservation of the casting "seams" which show the joins between the different foundry moulds, bears witness to the respect with which Rodin regarded his "trade" and to his preoccupation with making his viewing public aware of his technique.

Also in this room, several other single figures and groups illustrate Rodin's ideas for the complex project *The Gates of Hell* which was to tell in the form of allegory of the sufferings of the human soul (see also: ROOMS 9 and 10 and the GARDENS). *Eve and the Serpent*, in marble, was also entitled *Temptation*. *The Centauress*, half human, half animal, also called *Body and Soul*, symbolizes the duality of spirit and instinct. *Psyche*, without evoking a precise episode of the famous legend, embodies feminine beauty. The same sensual atmosphere pervades the group *Orpheus and the Maenads* in which Orpheus, having lost his wife Eurydice, is in the clutches of Dionysus's frenzied acolytes. In two other groups, *The Wave* and *The Poet and the Siren*, chisel marks make them look unfinished and spontaneous. On the mantelpiece, *Study of a woman* is the portrait of the classical beauty, Marianne Russell (see also ROOM 4, *Pallas and the Parthenon*), treated as a homage to Greek Antiquity.

General view

The Duchesse de Choiseul, Lady Sackville-West

ROOM 8. This room shows a series of female portraits executed after 1900 when a big one-man show had brought Rodin international fame. Considering the rather restricted possibilities of this kind of commissioned work, Rodin manages to bring astonishing variety to his portraits: each bust is very definitely not only a likeness but the expression of a personality. The handsome Englishwoman Eve Fairfax is forcefully fully frontal. On the other hand, Lady Sackville-West is asleep, her languid head resting on a pillow of rough marble. The same dreamy quality pervades the portrait of Madame Fenaille, the wife of a faithful and helpful friend of Rodin's, who became an important benefactor and then subsequently director of the museum. The poetic quality of these works contrasts with the bust of the formidable Duchesse de Choiseul who was Rodin's very provocative and crafty mastermind from 1905 to 1911: her image seems to bear witness that a vivacious smile cannot necessarily hide the avarice of the sitter. The group *Mother with a Dying Child*, commissioned for the tomb of Mrs Thomas Merrill's daughter, is overtly influenced by a painting of *Mother and Child* by Eugène Carrière: the two artists mutually respected each other's capacity for expressing motherly love without falling into sentimentality. Mrs Potter-Palmer was a very wealthy American, who living between Chicago and Paris, encouraged and financed exhibitions of women artists.

And Anglo-Saxons were not the only clients to request sittings from the Master! Madame de Goloubeff, the Caucasian translator and Muse of Gabriele d'Annunzio, and Madame Elisseieff, whose bust in marble carved by Despiau, under the supervision of Rodin, is at the Hermitage Museum in Saint Petersburg, are both exhibited here. *The Slav Woman*, which dominates the middle of the room, received its title at a later date and probably portrays the Czech artist Braunerova whose very distinctive features inspired Rodin on several other occasions.

The Slav Woman

Nude woman sitting

Cambodian Dancer

Illustration for *Le jardin des Supplices* by
Octave Mirbeau

Dance Movement

DRAWINGS ROOM. Visitors usually are not aware that there are over seven thousand drawings in the museum's collection left to the State by Rodin at the same time as the sculpture bequest.

Because of their number, they are exhibited in rotation, every three months, and are dimly lit for conservation purposes. Although using the same themes as the sculpture and capturing the sense of volume fundamental in a sculptor's work, Rodin's drawings represented a totally independent activity and are often an interpretation after a sculpture rather than a preparatory study for one. Depending on their visit, visitors will be able to discover early works, often copies after Antiquity or the Renaissance, gouaches and wash drawings for Dante's *Inferno*, studies for sculpture in pencil and pen and ink, portraits, and especially countless images of women, occasionally heightened in gouache or watercolour, often in movement and in extremely free and daring poses.

Crouching draped woman

Cambodian Dancer

Saint John the Baptist; to the left: *The Walking Man;* to the right: *Bust of Rodin* by J. Dubois

HALLWAY AND STAIRCASE. The entrance hall is dominated by two over-life-size figures: *Saint John the Baptist*, a favourite but usually insipidly sentimental subject of nineteenth century sculpture, is an athletic and forceful figure with a very strong individuality more in tune with the charisma of the subject, and *The Walking Man*, which was long considered to be a study for the *Saint John*. The links between the two are in fact more complex because it was only in 1900 that Rodin exhibited this daring piece, headless and armless and whose walking movement is the essence of its subject; its feet solidly anchored to the ground but continuously on the move captures "Time in Motion" much as Boccioni and the Futurists in Italy would try to do a few years later.

Halfway up the grand staircase, a visitor will first encounter *The Three Shades*, a smaller version of the three figures placed at the top of *The Gates of Hell*: overwhelmed with grief, the three figures seem to embody in art form Dante's description of Hell: "Abandon all hope, you who enter here!" Composed of three identical assembled figures, but in such a lively way that the spectator never realizes it, they totally avoid monotony and symmetry. This repetition of figures within a composition is an innovative "trade-mark" of the artist.

A little higher up the staircase, one can see the ferocious *Bellona* which Rodin had submitted as an entry to a competition in 1879 for a bust epitomizing the Republic, and indeed the press at the time had remarked upon its originality and strength. However, it was not accepted by the jury because it did not represent the Republic as reassuringly calm and serene but as violent and warlike. Too obviously against the official image of a traditional theme,

Bust of Rodin by Bourdelle; *The Three Shades*

47

Rodin re-named his bust and exhibited it later as the goddess of war. There is little doubt that Rose Beuret posed for this sculpture.

On the first floor landing, the convulsed figure of *The Martyr* gives the visitor a taste of the studies for *The Gates of Hell* exhibited in the two next rooms (on the courtyard). This sculpture, sometimes called *The Christian Martyr*, although she seems to illustrate a passion more physical than religious, is a prime example of Rodin's tendency to confuse love and suffering. From the point of view of technique, it is the first sculpture not to rest on a formal base but directly on its presentation platform: this innovative way of eliminating the base was also used by Degas to give life and strength to his figures. *The Martyr* with added wings was re-employed in *Illusion Sister of Icarus*, illustrating Rodin's fondness for combining existing elements to create new compositions.

The Martyr

General view

ROOM 9. In this room, the visitor can view studies for *The Gates of Hell*, which Rodin was commissioned to design in 1880: it would have served as entrance to the new museum of decorative arts, planned near the present-day Musée d'Orsay but never built. Obviously, the *Gates* were never used and Rodin then exhibited separately bits of the composition and reliefs which were to cover the doors. Thus *The Gates of Hell* became an ideal excuse for Rodin to experiment with his novel "assemblage" techniques. The theme is taken from Dante's *Divine Comedy* in which the poet travels through the three realms of Hell, Purgatory and Paradise. Rodin doesn't try to describe these literally but uses the themes of passion and violence to express the conflicts, anguish and sadness in his own private life.

The Thinker is exhibited in its original size, as it was meant to sit at the centre of the *Gates*: often thought of as Minos, the Judge of Souls, or Dante the poet, or Rodin himself, the sculptor confronting his creation, it is more often than not simply thought of as the embodiment of Man as powerful intellect. A painting by the Norwegian artist Edvard Munch of *The Thinker in the Garden of Dr Linde in Lübeck* demonstrates the fact that this piece was very popular with collectors right from the start.

Several preparatory studies witness the complexity of the project: in particular, in the display cases, two wax models which are the very first ideas for the *Gates*: the first, a simplified geometric outline, the second, a tiny sketch in which the many figures are represented by thumbmarks in the

Study for *The Gates of Hell*

The Three Graces

wax. On the righthand wall, the visitor can see a more elaborate version in plaster where the figures and groupings are more recognizable.

In a display case, *The Kneeling Fauness*, whose face bears a wild look, represents physical beauty; *The Toilet of Venus* (outside the case) is a softened version of the former. *The Falling Man* betrays the influence of Michelangelo on Rodin during the 1880s. The *Torso of Adèle* is named after a familiar model whose sensuous forms he used frequently. *The Three Graces* is another example of repetition of three identical figures.

In the middle of the room, *The Prodigal Son* is the image of pain and distress, shown in the tense muscular contortions of the figure. The same tragic feeling emanates from *The Cry* and from *The Weeping Woman* in grey marble. In *Despair*, a feminine form is hunched up in a position probably inspired by ballet movements. *Meditation*, which was meant to be placed at the top righthand corner of the *Gates*, was used in several other compositions, in particular the fourth project for the Victor Hugo monument.

The Torso of Adèle

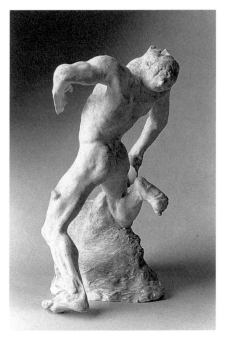

The Falling Man

The Prodigal Son

Study for *The Gates of Hell*

The Toilet of Venus

The Kneeling Fauness

I am Beautiful

ROOM 10. As in the previous room, the visitor can see more studies and figures for *The Gates of Hell*, to which Rodin gave lives of their own by casting them in bronze or carving them in marble. For instance, *Danaid*, who was forced to fill a bottomless barrel after having, with her sisters, slit her husband's throat on her wedding night, is a marvellously executed marble in a nervous and refined style.

The group *Fugit Amor*, also in marble, of which there were several versions executed after the plaster of 1887, illustrates the damnation of the adulterous lovers tormented by the winds of hell. Indeed, the couple seem to be propelled by an invisible force and the two figures back to back seem to be at once fleeing one another and stuck inexorably together. *Paolo and Francesca in the Clouds*, also known as *Paolo and Francesca in Torment*, also represents a couple of blighted adulterous lovers. *The Crouching Woman*, meant to be to the right of *The Thinker*, shows a woman in a very extreme position which baffled critics when Rodin exhibited the head on its own with its right cheek resting on the bent knee. Rodin assembled this figure with *The Falling Man* (in the previous room) and called it *I am Beautiful* after a poem by Baudelaire whose title is carved on the base. A drawing of the same subject by the artist illustrates a poem from *Les Fleurs du Mal* by this poet whose sombre poems particularly inspired him. Another poem, but this time by a fifteenth century poet, François Villon, inspired *She who was once the Helmet Maker's Beautiful Wife* whose ragged forms realistically describe

I am Beautiful

The Crouching Woman

the decay caused by old age. Two other sculptures, similar in theme, are shown near this masterpiece: *Clotho*, a plaster by Camille Claudel showing the cruel goddess of fate weaving man's destiny and *Misery* by Jules Desbois who was an accomplished sculptor in his own right as well as an assistant of Rodin.

The theme of *Ugolino*, the Pisan tyrant condemned to die in a dark cellar after having devoured the bodies of his own children who had died of starvation, was a frequent one in the nineteenth century. In a horizontal but very curvy composition, Rodin renews the treatment of this subject: his Ugolino is practically animal-like, with the dazed, absent look of someone who has lost all human conscience.

On the walls, several pictures from Rodin's own collection are exhibited: among them, the visitor can see the *Head of a wounded man* which has been attributed to Géricault in the past, a large still-life by Théodule Ribot and a landscape by Maximilien Luce which represents the gardens of Rodin's property in Meudon before the building which now houses his plasters was built.

Danaid

Camille Claudel: *Clotho*

Second sketch for *The Burghers of Calais*

ANTE-CHAMBER OF ROOM 11. Here, the visitor can see several small-scale bronzes such as *Fatigue*, *Venus*, a larger plaster version of which was used on the theatre set of Pierre Louÿs's play *Aphrodite*, and *Vain Tenderness*, a relief which reproduces the side pilaster of *The Gates of Hell*.

ROOM 11. This room is dedicated to Rodin's great composition *The Burghers of Calais*, which was commissioned in 1884 by the city of Calais to commemorate the celebrated episode of the Hundred Years War recounted in the chronicles of Froissart. The city, under siege by Edward III of England, was saved by six of its most eminent citizens who had offered to sacrifice their lives to save their city from destruction. Barefoot, in sackcloth robes and with ropes round their necks, they were about to be hanged on the main square had it not been for the intercession of the Queen, Philippa of Hainault. The Academic treatment of such a monument would have demanded a pyramidal composition dominated by a heroic figure and surrounded by pomp and allegory. Rodin refused this conventional approach, adopting the idea, from the very first "maquette", of a coherent group of six figures at the same level and of the same size which reinforces the notion of collective sacrifice. This small sketch was followed by a somewhat larger one a third of the size of the final life-size sculpture, and which studies each figure as a distinct personality facing death with courage, determination, resignation or despair in the robes of the condemned, through which the anatomy is visible. In fact, Rodin had studied each figure in the nude before clothing it and

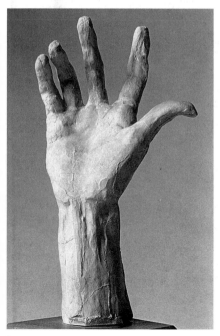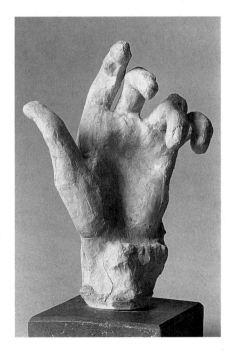

Studies of hands for *The Burghers of Calais*

many studies are here to prove it. He also made many studies of hands and individual faces and these are particularly vivid and personalized images.

Especially interesting is the larger than life *Head of Pierre de Wissant*, which was first exhibited in 1909 and which was no doubt inspired by the colossal examples of Hellenistic sculpture. The *Bust of Jean d'Aire* was transposed into glazed stoneware by Jeanneney in 1904: it confirms Rodin's interest in new techniques which were being evolved at the Sèvres factory at the time and where he worked from time to time (see: ROOM 2).

Apart from the individual studies of hands and heads, the showcase on the left contains an enigmatic pile of severed heads and members over which looms a winged figure taken from *The Gates of Hell*. This technique of combining different elements in an unexpected way or to misappropriate them in a surprising context was to become an important feature of modern sculpture: there is no doubt that Rodin was a pioneer of these revolutionary ideas.

Several copies of photographs show Rodin working on the *Burghers* and you may view the final sculpture in the gardens.

The visitor now returns to the landing and then turns right into the rooms facing the gardens to complete his tour of the museum.

Study for *The Gates of Hell*, assemblage of severed heads and hands

Study for *The Burghers of Calais: Jean d'Aire, nude*

Exhortation

ROOM 12. Because he pursued a policy of accepting large State commissions for important monuments and actively sought to exhibit whenever and wherever he could, Rodin was, from the very beginning of the century, famous worldwide. However, in this room, the visitor can see works that were created independently of any commissions or specific projects.

Several groups, whose titles are more poetic than descriptive, and which include *The Good Spirit*, *Spirits of Evil*, *Exhortation*, *Esculape*, are also pieces created by "assemblages" of separate figures. Contrary to the traditional and academic technique of sculpture where the artist starts from a specific pre-established idea, Rodin is much more interested in the relationship between forms and the balance between void and

object, only giving his work a title, often with help from his author friends, after it was finished. This is the case in the marble *The Shell and the Pearl*, whose title is just a poetic excuse to express the body of a woman, no doubt unfinished, extracting herself from a block of marble. In the centre of the room, the visitor can see *The Death of Adonis*, or *Venus and Adonis*, which evokes the legend of the young and handsome Adonis slaughtered by a wild boar and mourned by Venus who loved him. Another marble of the same subject is in ROOM 16.

The plaster *Beside the Sea* is the synthesis of several studies of seated or crouching bathers and the head of the Slav woman in ROOM 8. As if in contrast to the tormented atmosphere of *The Gates of Hell* which obsessed Rodin for many years, one feels that he

Before the Sea

is seeking the serenity of the classical sculpture of Greek and Roman Antiquity which he himself actively collected. "I constantly try to make my vision of Nature more peaceful", he wrote to his friend, the art critic Gustave Coquiot; that same quiet strength pervades *The American Athlete*, which depicts Samuel Stockton White. When Rodin asked him to choose a pose, he quite naturally and spontaneously took up the *Thinker*'s which Rodin then transposed in a more relaxed manner. More than twenty years separate the two works and the later sculpture is a much more balanced work. However, the persistent necessity for dramatic or tragic inspiration can still be seen in *The Storm* (known also as *Terror*) or *The Marathon Runner*.

The Storm

The American Athlete

Mozart or Portrait of Gustav Mahler

ROOM 13. The best pictures of Rodin's private collection are here. He not only received them as presents but bought hundreds of quality works of all styles and periods. For instance, *Le Père Tanguy* by Vincent van Gogh, represents the celebrated artist's materials vendor in Montmartre sitting against a backdrop of Japanese prints most of which are recognizable, and *The Viaduct in Arles*, with its subtle colour scheme, and *The Harvesters* with its daring composition are prime examples of Van Gogh's Provençal period. Renoir's *Female Nude* of 1880 demonstrates that he was the only Impressionist to retain the female form as a favourite artistic subject. The large canvas by Claude Monet, *Belle Isle*, is one of a series he painted in 1886 in Brittany on the theme of harmony between the rocks and the sea. They are also a poignant

testimony of the close friendship between the painter and the sculptor, born the same year, and often exhibited together (taking the year 1889 as an example, a mere 145 paintings and 35 sculptures!) The visitor should also examine the ten little oil sketches after Spanish masters by the sculptor Falguière and two portraits of Rodin by J.-P. Laurens and A. Legros. A curious Dutch chest, whose many drawers were probably meant to hold the coins of a money-changer, also belonged to Rodin.

Several sculpted busts show the many links Rodin had with the political, literary and artistic figures of his time. Clemenceau, the journalist who became a member of parliament, then minister of war in 1917, was not a happy commission for Rodin who disagreed thoroughly with the sitter's pol-

Anna de Noailles

Georges Clemenceau

itical opinions. The sitter, in turn, was exasperated by the eighteen sittings it took the sculptor to capture his likeness! Dissatisfied with the result, he forced Rodin to exhibit it anonymously. However, despite Clemenceau's criticism of the work, it does indeed capture his enigmatic and disdainful force of character. Etienne Clémentel is no doubt the last personality to have posed for Rodin, whom he helped greatly with the creation of his museum: he had founded the International Chamber of Commerce and occupied several important political posts during his long and distinguished career.

The painter Puvis de Chavannes, renowned for his large allegorical murals, and the sculptor Falguière are both bronzes of great psychological depth. The marble entitled *Mozart* is in fact the transposition of the portrait

Van Gogh, *Portrait of Père Tanguy, The Viaduct in Arles*. Renoir: *Female Nude*

of the composer Gustav Mahler executed in 1909. Here again, Rodin uses the "formula" of contrasting the roughness of the marble with the silky smoothness of the face of the model, avoiding all Academic stereotypes.

Another marble represents George Bernard Shaw, the great Irish playwright and polemist who, although not renowned for his generosity towards other artists, wrote to Rodin: "I am forever proud of being known as your model; you are the only man who makes me feel truly humble." Other writers are exhibited in this room including the playwright Henri Becque and the poet Anna de Noailles who thought her portrait was so unflattering that she nearly cancelled her sittings.

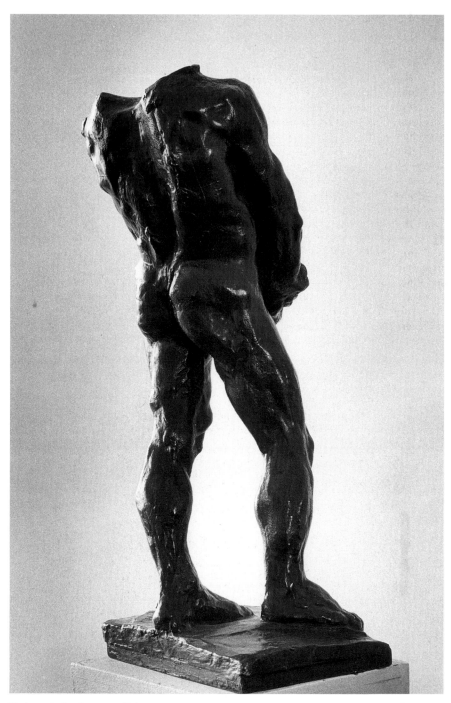

Nude study for the statue *Balzac*

ROOM 14. The works shown here are related to the large public commissions. Some are not particularly large scale, such as *Last Vision*, a relief in the symbolist style dedicated to the poet Maurice Rollinat and composed of the head of *The Slav Woman*, a study for the head of *Saint John the Baptist* and some hands.

Others are more traditional, such as the sketch for the *Monument to Claude Lorrain* in Nancy, showing the painter on a pedestal from which Apollo and his horses appear, as if to symbolize the sunlight and general luminosity that pervades the artist's work.

Some other projects were never executed, for instance, the 1905 commission to commemorate the American painter Whistler; all we know about this project is the bronze of *The Muse of Inspiration* and the *Head of a Muse*

in marble, for which Gwen John, the English artist-sister of Augustus John and occasional mistress of Rodin, posed.

Several sculptures relate to the monument to Victor Hugo. It was supposed to be included in a vast decorative project dedicated to the great men of France in the Panthéon in Paris. Rodin already had a likeness of the poet because he had sculpted his bust in 1883 but with great difficulty as he refused to sit long enough. A first series of sketches show *Victor Hugo Sitting on the Rocks of Exile*, that is of Guernsey, but this was not considered in accordance with the official programme so he changed it into *The Apotheosis of Victor Hugo* in which the great man is seen standing in contemporary clothes and surrounded by allegorical figures exalting the epic qualities of his poetry.

Nude studies for the statue *Balzac*

Penultimate draped study for the statue *Balzac*

Among these are the three Nereids, or *Voices of the Sea* which came directly from *The Three Sirens* on *The Gates of Hell* (see also in the GARDENS, the Monument to Victor Hugo called *of the Palais-Royal*).

Many studies for the monument to Balzac punctuate the long elaboration of a work considered by some as a major step in modern sculpture and by others as a terrible failure. It was commissioned in 1891 by the Société des Gens de Lettres of which Balzac was the second president. Rodin began by collecting information on the physical and sartorial characteristics of the novelist, although, of course, he had been dead over forty years. He first did a series of pretty lifelike studies, the *Bust of the Young Balzac* for example, taken from a portrait by the painter Devéria, nude and studies *Balzac in a Dominican robe*.

However, after a long period away from the project, Rodin abandoned the realist tendency and gave way to a much more daring and un-naturalistic image of the poet, very much simplified and magnificently swathed, as in the penultimate draped study, thus expressing the genius and the larger-than-life quality of the author of *La Comédie Humaine* (see also: the final version of the monument in the GARDENS). On the walls, the visitor can see several counter-proofs of photographs by the American photographer Edward Steichen which show the installation of the large plaster of Balzac in Rodin's garden in Meudon.

Nereids

Bathers, for the decoration of a swimming-pool

ROOM 15. Three series of works can be seen in this room: purely decorative projects, and sculptures on the themes of the hand and of dance. Several marbles, such as *The Little Water Fairy* and its variant *Flowers in a Vase* and *Fish Woman* are most probably sketches for fountains. *Bacchus in the Vat*, also known as *The Faun*, was probably meant as a garden sculpture. In a fireplace designed for the South American tycoon, Don Matias Errazuriz, Rodin reduced his *Adam and Eve* from *The Gates of Hell* and used them for the uprights. At the end of the nineteenth century, he was involved in the Art Nouveau movement with many of his contemporaries, and with Falguière, Bracquemond, Chéret and Charpentier in particular, he provided designs for the Villa La Sapinière at Evian, which belonged to the sister of one of

his patrons, Baron Vitta. There are two large plasters for planters decorated with playing *putti* on the theme of the harvest and grape-picking. With the four *Bathers* in terracotta which were to stand in niches around the swimming-pool at the Neuilly residence of one of Rodin's rich patrons, Maurice Fenaille, we see how much Rodin was influenced by the new trends of Art Nouveau in the sinuous and curvy treatment of the models.

For him, hands were as expressive as faces and could convey emotions, ideas and even personality. *Lovers' Hands* is composed of two right hands, a woman's and a man's, to symbolize the embrace of two lovers. *Hand from the Tomb* takes a hand already used in *The Burghers of Calais* but reversed, and was probably conceived as a funeral monument and, as with many of

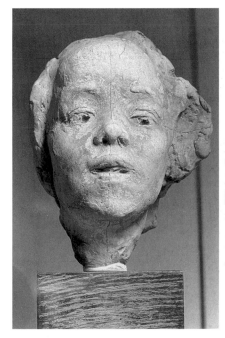

Studies after the Japanese dancer *Hanako*

Dance Movements

Rodin's later works, was given several titles including *Punishment*, *Spirit of the Dead*, *Pharès (omen of death)* and *Thecel* which gave the piece a more sinister meaning.

Movement being the essence of Rodin's art, he was naturally attracted to dance and ballet. As early as 1910, he sculpted a series of small figurines called *Dance Movements* which describe much more complicated and acrobatic postures than the conventional classical ballet movements. Limbering up and stretching exercises are expressed by arbitrary distortion of the anatomy of the figures. The smallest sculpture represents Nijinsky whom he had admired with the Ballets Russes in Paris in 1912 dancing *L'Après-Midi d'un Faune*. Finally, the visitor must note two terracotta studies of Hanako, the Japanese dancer, whose extraordinary face inspired Rodin to sculpt her fifty-three times.

Dancer, also called *Nijinsky*

The Little Water Fairy

Nymph Games, behind: *Psyche-Spring*, to the right: *The Creation of Woman*

ROOM 16. In this space can be seen bronzes and marbles on the theme of man and woman often disguised by mythological or literary titles, in which Rodin depicts physical passion without falling into vulgarity or triviality. *The Minotaur*, or *Jupiter the Bull* as it is sometimes called, is one of the numerous works inspired by Ovid's *Metamorphoses*: its double title allows two interpretations, either it is Jupiter in the form of a white bull ravishing Europa, who will conceive Minos, King of Crete, or it could be construed as the monster son of Minos and Pasiphae who, every seven years, was sent seven virgins and seven young men to consume until he was killed by Theseus. Its free and sensuous composition reminds us of the art of the eighteenth century which we know Rodin admired greatly. The bull's head reappears in *Pygmalion and Galatea* which symbolizes the myth of the sculptor in love with his sculpted form which is brought to life by Aphrodite. Here again, the inspiration is Ovid, but also the eighteenth century whose artists often took this theme. Ovid also told the story of poor Psyche persecuted by the jealous Aphrodite, and Rodin was very taken by this subject although one cannot clearly understand the theme of *Psyche-Spring*, sometimes called *Surprised Nymph*, a title which in fact seems more appropriate. Among the many other sculptures inspired by mythology, *Bacchante* or *Nymphs' Games* for instance, most works are composed of "assemblages" of earlier pieces: this method allows Rodin to use the countless figures, in different sizes and contexts, which he had created for *The Gates of Hell* and give them a completely new meaning.

The Death of Adonis illustrates more successfully than does the marble in Room 12 the myth of the cycles of nature: one can see on the righthand side of the work the handsome adolescent's drops of blood turned into anemones. Other mythical compositions, such as *Embracing Bacchantes*, *Triton and a Nereid on a Dolphin* and *The Fall of Icarus* are only pretexts to use the serpentine lines of Art Nouveau, but *The Creation of Woman* is surprising in the apparent imbalance between the massive and uncentred base, representing a cloud from which springs the arm of God.

Psyche-Spring

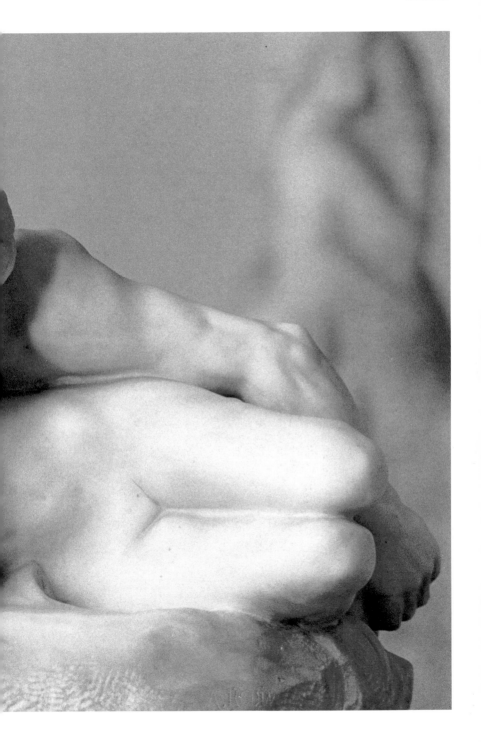

The Thinker

THE COURTYARD
AND THE GARDENS

The courtyard was once surrounded by service buildings necessary for the management of a large household. They were refurbished and enlarged during the nineteenth century to satisfy the needs of the Convent of the Sacred Heart who also built several chapels in the convent grounds. The largest still survives and borders the Rue de Varenne: it is a Neo-Gothic building by the architect Lisch, built between 1875 and 1876, and for the last twenty years used as an exhibition hall for temporary exhibitions although it might be assigned a different use in a future reorganization of the museum quarters under discussion as we write.

To the right of the courtyard, *The Thinker* stands out against the silhouetted dome of the church of Saint-Louis des Invalides. It must be remembered that, although this piece has acquired a fame all of its own, it was supposed to surmount *The Gates of Hell* (see: ROOM 9). Its immediate success drove Rodin to enlarge it by a new method derived from the pantograph. It has become the Image of the Creator across the world and is one of the works of art that everyone recognizes. This bronze was cast by public subscription and was to be placed in front of the Panthéon but was considered too small and was transferred to the gardens of the museum in 1922.

Skirting round the Hôtel to the right, one comes across the large figure of *Balzac*. The plaster, which was exhibited at the Salon of 1898, had been badly received by the public who were not expecting the effigy of a famous man

in which likeness and reality had given way to visionary invention.

With this figure, Rodin breaks with all the past formulas used by other sculptors to honour great men. Preferring to stress the interior battles of the author, he has him striding in a fiercely proud and defiant attitude, swathed in an ill-fitting coat which gives definition to the highly lined face, itself the expression of creative genius. It really is the beginning of modern sculpture as we know it today.

To the left of the courtyard, *The Burghers of Calais* is one of eleven casts which are dispersed worldwide, the first of which was unveiled in Calais in 1895. Comparing this to the preparatory studies already seen in ROOM 11, the dramatic qualities are accentuated in the final version, especially in the faces and in the complicated patterns created by the draperies. The sculpture, being presented at ground level, "very low so that the spectators can penetrate the heart of the subject", as Rodin himself put it, strengthens the feeling of the prisoners' march towards death.

The Gates of Hell lean against the wall which separates these gardens from the neighbouring property, which was in the eighteenth century the residence of the Duchesse de Maine's steward. Rodin worked on the *Gates* from 1880 until the end of his life, but with long interruptions while he worked on other projects as he was not one to completely finish one project before beginning another: indeed working on several ideas at once seemed to stimulate his imagination. The organization

Balzac

of the assembly of all its parts was one of Rodin's last tasks but he never lived to see it cast in bronze: the five existing casts were posthumous and one can be seen in Paris, two in the United States, one in Switzerland and one, and hopefully a second soon, in Japan.

In his first attempts, Rodin had been inspired by the bronze doors of the Italian Renaissance, in particular Ghiberti's "gates of Paradise" for the Baptistry in Florence with their panels divided into squares, but he quite quickly turned to a composition abounding in figures which burst out of the architectural framework. It conjures up all the torments of Hell. The lintel at the top is an extraordinary three layers of figures in high relief, as they are to be seen from below (the doors are 6.35m high!) Boldly moulded, the multitude of figures behind *The Think-*

The Burghers of Calais

The Burghers of Calais, Jean d'Aire

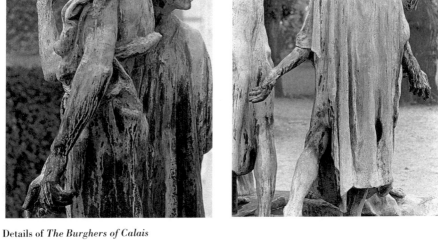

Details of *The Burghers of Calais*

The Gates of Hell

er are in fact all falling to the right. A skeleton surrounded by a frieze of little severed heads calls to mind the famous medieval *danses macabres* and reinforces the underlying theme of death.

The two doors are framed by low-relief sculpted pilasters. The figures seem to be smothered and deformed by their background and invoke suffering and pain. As for the doors themselves, they are covered with more than a hundred and fifty figures linked in attitudes of a daring unknown to sculpture until then. Because of the physical seriousness and technical grandeur of the project, Rodin felt free to compose a work which breaks all traditional rules and to compose a new sculptural space very sensitive to light changes. A work without precedent or indeed successor, the *Gates* is very much Art Nouveau in its sinuous forms, *fin de siècle* in the

pessimism of its vision but very *avant garde* in its formal discoveries, never ceasing to fascinate and confound the spectator. The two monumental figures of Adam and Eve on either side only add to the general pathos.

The Gates of Hell, lower part of the left-hand door

The Gates of Hell, details

MARBLE GALLERY. To the right of the *Gates*, a covered gallery shelters several marbles of too considerable a size and weight to exhibit inside the museum and those which remain unfinished. For the large work entitled *Ariadne* which was meant to be a funeral monument but remained unfinished because of the First World War, Rodin used a well-known model, Mrs Abruzzezzi, after whom the piece is often named. *The Genius of Eternal Rest* was meant for a large monument to Puvis de Chavannes in the Panthéon. The roughing out of this piece was done by several assistants but taken over by Charles Despiau, who was to become one of the famous sculptors of the next generation, but he himself gave up because of the Great War. Of the unfinished pieces exhibited here, *The Spring* is interesting as it shows how Rodin tried to "personalize" the elements: clouds, water, rocks. It also retains the nails buried in plaster where the apparatus used to transpose a plaster into a marble of the same size has been attached. Other unfinished marbles are *Night and Day*, a fight between a woman and a man, *Niobid* and several portraits such as *Head of a Muse for the Whistler Monument*, Clemenceau and Madame Fenaille. On the other hand, there are very explicit texts which confirm that the large busts of Puvis de Chavannes and Victor Hugo, both freely executed and in a symbolist vein, were in fact completely finished. Opposite the Marble Gallery, *The Three Shades* was cast from a greatly enlarged plaster in 1898 which reinforces the influence of Michelangelo.

Behind the Hôtel, you will find the Gardens, in which several more works are exhibited.

The Three Shades

Cybela

On the south-facing terrace at the rear of the building, two *Caryatides* face each other: these are enlargements of figures from the *Gates* in which Rodin renews the classical theme of a figure holding up a large weight: instead of the stately and impassive figure that one would find in Greek Antiquity, Rodin's is painfully overwhelmed by his burden.

Under the terrace, the *Muse for the Whistler Monument* is an enlargement of the study exhibited inside in ROOM 14. She is naked, her leg against a rock symbolizing Fame, her ample forms reminding one of Maillol's works. This is also the case for *Cybela* opposite, yet again a much enlarged version of a little figure from the *Gates* whose title denotes the goddess of vegetation and nature and whose model was the same as that used for *Eve* and *Ariadne*.

In the undergrowth to the left of the central lawn, one can see several bronzes of four figures of *The Burghers of Calais* dressed as well as life-size studies in the nude for the same group.

Further on, one comes across the *Victor Hugo Monument* called *of the Palais-Royal*: this is the marble commissioned in 1891 after one of his sketches for the Panthéon monument but this time meant for the Luxembourg Gardens. Represented as a naked hero, Victor Hugo finished up in the gardens of the Palais-Royal where he remained until 1933. Unfortunately, the pile of rocks which served as a base to the sculpture and which was intended to symbolize the rocks of Guernsey where he was exiled has disappeared.

In the middle of the central ornamental pond, there is an enlargement of *Ugolino* (see also ROOM 10) and surrounding it several large-scale bronzes: *Eve, The Great Shade, Meditation*, all from the *Gates*, as well as *The Genius of Eternal Rest* (see also the MARBLE GALLERY).

At the bottom of the gardens is the enlargement of *The Call to Arms* which was cast on the instruction of Rodin in 1912 from the project which one can see in ROOM 3.

Coming back towards the Hôtel Biron to the left, one finds the statue of the painter Claude Lorrain, on the same theme as the monument to the painter in Nancy (see ROOM 14) and that of Bastien-Lepage, a realist painter of the time: both stand, palette in hand, "on the motif", in natural poses.

The Greek and Roman antiquities, mostly torsos and sculptures, scattered about the gardens all come from Rodin's private collection.

Two nude studies for *The Burghers of Calais, Pierre de Wissant*

Two *Burghers of Calais: Eustache de Saint-Pierre* in the foreground and *Andrius d'Andres*

Rodin in his studio, in front of the base of the monument to the President of Argentina, *Sarmiento*

THE BIOGRAPHY OF RODIN

François-Auguste René Rodin was born on 12th November 1840 in Paris in what is now the fifth arrondissement. His parents were of peasant stock, from Eastern France, but his father had had a moderately successful career in the police force. The young Auguste went to the local school and then, from 1851 to 1853, to the boarding school owned by his paternal uncle in Beauvais, in Northern France. His academic results were disappointing, perhaps because of undetected short-sightedness, but he always showed an aptitude for drawing. In 1854, this talent became a vocation when he entered the École Impériale Spéciale de Dessin et de Mathématiques, also known as the "Petite École" as opposed to the École des Beaux-Arts, known as the "Grande École". In this establishment, which was free of charge, students were taught mainly technical drawing since they would mostly become craftsmen and decorators in the applied arts (the fashion at the time was for highly decorated interiors and buildings). Rodin took lessons in architectural drawing, drawing after Greek and Roman sculpture, stone carving and modelling under a remarkable teacher Lecocq de Boisbaudran who also taught him to exercise his visual memory by sending him to make copies at the Louvre and the Bibliothèque Impériale.

At seventeen and then again at eighteen, he tried unsuccessfully to get into the École des Beaux-Arts. His friend Dalou the sculptor, who was himself a pupil there although he never obtained the "Prix de Rome", later congratulated him for having thus avoided being indoctrinated by official art.

He then spent several years working for building contractors where, for five francs a day, he would mix the plaster and prepare moulds while studying animal anatomy at the zoo in the Jardin des Plantes and human anatomy from models at the Gobelins at night.

In 1862, the death of his eldest sister Maria, who had entered a convent after an unsuccessful love affair with a friend of Rodin's Arthur Barnouvin, brought about in him a mystical crisis and he himself entered, as a novice, the Order of the Fathers of the Very Holy Sacrament, a newly formed congregation founded on abnegation and self-sacrifice. Very quickly, the founder of the Order, the Reverend Father Eymard, who posed for a bust by Rodin which he found a little "diabolical", encouraged him to return to his artistic career.

In 1864, the Salon's refusal of Rodin's *The Man With the Broken Nose* was a terrible disappointment as it was, at that time, the only real way for an artist to be properly recognized. He also made the acquaintance that year of an eighteen year old seamstress, Rose Beuret, who was virtually illiterate but plucky and attractive and who remained by his side with the loyalty "of an animal", as he would say, until the end of their lives. They had a son in 1866 but Rodin never acknowledged him and he died a pauper in 1934.

At this time, he started working for Carrier-Belleuse, a very fashionable sculptor of the era: in his studio, he soon became a "figure-maker" which involved sculpting figures as well as ornament. During the Franco-Prussian War and the Paris Commune, Carrier-Belleuse was forced to transfer his workshops to Brussels, a prosperous artistic centre where the mayors Anspach and Brouckère had already started ambitious town-planning. Rodin, who had volunteered in 1870 for the National Guard but was declared unfit for service because of bad eyesight shortly afterwards, went straight to join Carrier-Belleuse in Brussels, leaving Rose and his small son behind although they joined him the following year.

During his seven years in Brussels, Rodin collaborated on several big projects, which have nearly all survived to this day, including the Stock Exchange, the Palace of the Academies and the Royal Music Academy.

He fell out with Carrier-Belleuse for trying to sell his sculptures under his own name which was strictly forbidden in his contract and instead went into partnership with the Belgian sculptor Joseph van Rasbourg with whom he produced everything from little decorative statuettes cast in unlimited editions by the Brussels Bronze Company to large decorative projects. He was most probably the last great sculptor to have such versatile beginnings !

In the winter of 1875-1876, he journeyed to Italy, poverty forcing him to make part of his way on foot, to see Turin, Genoa, Rome, Naples, Siena but especially Florence where he studied Michelangelo from the originals instead of plaster casts. He wrote to Rose: "I think this great Magician has rubbed off on me a little".

The accusation, during the Salon of 1877, of his having moulded *The Bronze Age* directly on a model notwithstanding, he returned to Paris determined to concentrate on a personal and independent career while ignoring the official criteria. He started taking part in competitions for public monuments which became more and more frequent but, because of the originality of his ideas, he invariably failed to obtain the commissions, and so pursued his career as a "master builder in art", as he called himself, creating, for instance, large medallions to go on the fountains designed by Legrain in the new Trocadéro Palace, rebuilt for the Exposition Universelle of 1878.

He also worked on designs for the Sèvres porcelain factory and it was there that he befriended Maurice Haquette who was the brother-in-law of a secretary of state for the arts, Edmond Turquet. It was through him that in 1880, when he was already forty years old, Rodin received the commission for *The Gates of Hell*, on which he worked all his life. This commission led to his being given, by the government, a first, then a second more spacious studio within the Dépôt des Marbres in the Rue de l'Université.

He started to frequent some of the literary and political "salons" of the time and kept a sharp eye on the press's reaction to his work. In 1881, the year the *Saint John the Baptist* was purchased by the State, he travelled for the first time to London where his college friend Alphonse Legros was a professor at the Slade and there learnt the technique of drypoint etching, which he put to good use over the next few years, producing a series of thirteen masterly prints. This first trip to London marks the beginning of a special relationship with England and the English, in particular with the critic Henley of the *Magazine of Art* who never ceased to praise Rodin's work.

During the years 1882-1884, he began some of the series of portraits of well-known sitters, who did not always approve of his realistic portrayal, which he executed throughout his long career.

In 1882, he lost his father (his mother had probably died as early as 1871), and met Camille Claudel who was twenty four years his junior and had an invincible ambition to become a great sculptress: he came by a combination of circumstances to look at her work as well as that of the three girlfriends with whom she shared a studio. During the ten years that their stormy affair lasted, Camille became his confidante, collaborator, disciple and model as well as his mistress and was thoroughly involved not only in his private but in his public life, which was chronicled by the Goncourt brothers.

Apart from the interminable *Gates*, Rodin was keen to get other commissions as working as a sculptor was a very expensive venture: there were the costly materials, the many assistants' salaries, the studios and warehouses to stock the overlarge pieces which were part and parcel of an important sculptor's entourage. *The Burghers of Calais*, which was commissioned in 1884 but only unveiled in 1895 because of financial wranglings, is a good example of the difficulties which Rodin kept on encountering. In 1887, he executed the monument to Bastien-Lepage and in 1889 he won the commission to sculpt the monument to Claude Lorrain, unveiled in 1892 in Nancy by President Sadi Carnot; also in 1889 Rodin started the monument to Victor Hugo which was supposed to be placed in the Panthéon but ended up, seventeen years later, in the Palais-Royal gardens.

In 1891, thanks to the Société des Gens de Lettres and Émile Zola in particular, he received the commission to execute a statue of Balzac, the plaster of which he exhibited at the Salon de la Société nationale des Beaux-Arts. This was judged totally scandalous and refused outright by the Society when, at the same exhibition, a marble of his, *The Kiss*, received rave reviews. While Rodin travelled around in Touraine to do extensive research on Balzac, Camille was at Azay-le-Rideau, probably recovering after an abortion.

His last public commission, executed between 1894 and 1899, was in Buenos Aires, of President Sarmiento of Argentina, who instituted public education for all in his country.

The next twenty years were especially productive and, apart from the *Gates*, Rodin was ever active in different ways: he illustrated many famous texts, for instance Baudelaire's *Fleurs du Mal* for the editor Gallimard in 1887 and *Le Jardin des Supplices* by Octave Mirbeau in 1899. His drawings were published in album form for the first time in 1897 which is always known as the *Goupil* Album after the helio-engraver who engraved 142 drawings on 129 plates. He exhibited frequently (with Georges Petit in 1889, for instance, with his friend Claude Monet), but somehow exhibitions only aggravated his fear of failure and his hunger for sales because he had the feeling that he must forever make money and yet was constantly out of pocket: he only gave 25F to the public subscription towards the purchase of Manet's *Olympia* by the Louvre !

However, public recognition came when he was made a "Chevalier" of the Légion d'Honneur in 1887, "Officier" in 1892 and "Commandeur" in 1903.

He was a member of the Exposition Universelle jury in 1889 and in the same year had founded a dissident group of artists, called the Société nationale des Beaux-Arts, to fight the conservative elements in charge of the official Salon. He took charge of the sculpture section in 1893.

His private life was less successful as he was being torn between his passion for Camille Claudel and his lasting affection for Rose, who, although she had not followed his social ascension into high society, had remained faithful through thick and thin while efficiently running his household and his large studio.

Camille had always believed that marriage was a possible outcome of her relationship with Rodin and moreover felt it unfair to be called his pupil when she considered herself to be his equal. She proceeded to leave him and the Folie Neubourg, a dilapidated but exquisite eighteenth century folly which had been their "love nest". Rodin, depressed and in ill-health, also left Paris for Meudon, firstly in the Bellevue quarter, then at the Villa des Brillants, a Napoleon III residence in the Louis XIII style, where he installed his workshops and where he would eventually die.

After the final breaking off of their liaison, Camille Claudel pursued her career alone but, Rodin's indirect help notwithstanding, was not successful and descended into dire misery and finally insanity. Critics have often reproached Rodin for not having tried to stop her being certified and interned in 1913 but fifteen years had passed since they had split up !

In 1900 he was sixty and had achieved world-wide acclaim: indeed, in the Exposition Universelle of 1900, he had a personal showing of 170 sculptures and drawings in a special building on the Place de l'Alma. A lithographic poster by his friend Eugène Carrière and a fully illustrated catalogue prefaced by Carrière, Laurens and Monet were published for this occasion and thanks to the very modern public relations techniques employed, Rodin made a large enough profit from the show to ease his up to then precarious financial situation.

From then on, he was asked to exhibit constantly: two thirds of the foreign shows were organized after 1900, for instance in Dusseldorf and Leipzig in 1904. In the Alma Pavilion which he had rebuilt in the grounds of his property in Meudon, he received the crowned heads of Europe and elsewhere who could choose from the plaster casts on show which bronze or marble they wanted to commission. On top of this, he was solicited for more and more portraits, to take on official duties which he enjoyed doing and to appear at social gatherings and events. He employed a large staff of sculptors including Bourdelle, Desbois, Despiau, Pompon and the Schnegg brothers who ran his workshops while he was occupied by ephemeral projects like the short-lived Rodin Academy, and he travelled worldwide to promote his work. He also started several abortive projects such as a *Tower of Work* and monuments to Puvis de Chavannes and Whistler, who had been the previous president of the International Society of Painters, Printers and Sculptors.

In the last ten years of his life, he made smaller and smaller works, portraits and dancing figures and drawings in which he concentrated on the feminine form. In 1906, he was fascinated by the dancers of the Cambodian king Sisowath who had come to Marseille to appear at the Exposition Coloniale and captured their swirling movements in subtle watercolours.

From 1905 to 1911, his liaison with the Duchesse de Choiseul surrounds him with intrigue and he fell out with many of his closest friends. However, the duchess, of American extraction, introduced him to many new clients from the United States where she asked Loïe Fuller, the dancer, to represent his interests. This resulted in a large number of Rodin's works entering American collections and eventually the opening of the Philadelphia Rodin Museum.

In 1905 and 1906, the poet Rainer-Maria Rilke, who had already published a book about Rodin in 1903, became his private secretary. He was soon to be dismissed "like a flunkey" by the sculptor who had become secretive and suspicious but by dint of patience and admiration for the great man, Rilke managed a reconciliation, and it is because of Rilke that Rodin came to the Hôtel Biron.

Henceforth, his fame and fortune were made: he was made Doctor "Honoris Causa" of the University of Jena in 1905, then came Oxford in 1907 and he was made "Grand Officier" of the Légion d'Honneur in 1910. To celebrate his seventieth birthday, the Japanese literary magazine *Shirakaba* published a special edition: to thank them, he sent three bronzes which remain to this day in the Kurashiki Museum.

In 1911, the British government purchased a cast of *The Burghers of Calais* to place in Westminster's Parliament gardens. The same year, several texts were published on or by him, including *Entretiens sur l'Art* compiled by Paul Gsell, *Conversations* with Dujardin-Baumetz and in 1914, *Les Cathédrales de France*, which were his own reflections on Gothic art of which he was so fond.

At the outset of the First World War, he left for England with Rose and Judith Cladel, his biographer, but soon returned to Paris and then travelled to Rome with Rose to sculpt Pope Benedict XV's bust "in situ", but he found the sitter impatient and intolerant of his political ideas which he expounded during the sittings.

Several strokes weakened him intellectually and, surrounded by greedy female admirers, but supported by his old faithful friends, not least Etienne Clémentel, Minister for Commerce, Rodin was at last able to see the three donations of his work enter into the national collections with the imminent creation of a museum dedicated to his art and his collections in mind.

He felt then that it was time to marry Rose which he did on 29th January 1917, in the Villa des Brillants, freezing cold through wartime lack of coal, before the Mayor of Meudon in the sitting room cum studio. Rose died on 14th February and Rodin survived until 17th November when he died of pneumonia brought on by the cold. Ironically, his death coincided with a shameful and shady maneouvre to enter the Institut without a proper election which would have been contrary to all his principles but thankfully he never lived to see it.

The couple are buried in the grounds of the Villa des Brillants under a large cast of *The Thinker*.

RODIN'S SCULPTURE TECHNIQUES

At the beginning of all Rodin's sculpture is the modelling of the subject in clay: this sketch, generally to be transposed in a different medium whether it be plaster, bronze or marble, is worked on for long periods at a time, and between working sessions the piece is covered in damp cloths to keep it moist and to avoid breakage. These clay models are worked with tools, of which none have survived, or more often with the sculptor's hands and this is why we can frequently see fingerprints in the clay.

Once the satisfactory result has been achieved in clay, a plaster mould of it is taken. This first mould taken directly from the model is called "creux perdu" as the mould is then broken open giving a unique piece called the "original plaster" which will be used instead of the clay model during the casting.

The only clay pieces that survive are those that have been fired at very high temperatures (600 to 1200 degrees Celcius).

Rodin was especially attached to the circulation of his works and this of course involved reproducing them. This is why he had made, from original plasters, moulds in several pieces called "moules à bon creux", from which he could obtain several plaster casts quite faithful to the original model which could then be used to cast the bronzes.

Casting techniques are complicated and numerous but can be loosely divided into two types: the "lost wax technique", which involves a wax model that melts as the kiln heats up and is replaced by the molten bronze, and "sand casting", which is especially used for large-scale pieces and whose mould is of sand in which the molten bronze is poured.

At the time, sculptors did not restrict the number of bronzes they would cast of one subject, but responded to demand, and that meant casting as many as possible. Rodin employed thirty foundry workers, often lowly artisans. There are also posthumous casts: these were cast from original plasters by the Rodin Museum as legal heirs to the sculptor's copyright. These casts are limited to an edition of twelve.

As far as the marbles are concerned, Rodin adopted the practice of the times by employing stonemasons, like Bourdelle, Despiau, Desbois and Pompon, who became famous in their own right, to carve most of the piece, only finishing it off himself. Indeed, Rodin never lost touch with the work, which he supervised constantly, as the archives and the unfinished pieces annotated in his hand confirm.